BY JOLENE

A Curious Book
by the
Nonsensical Therapist
vol 1

Challenge your thoughts, change your world,
because sometimes, nonsense makes the most sense.
A Curious Book

Dedication

This dedication might seem a little odd, but then again, I like odd! I'm a big fan of the cadence of Dr. Seuss, who has shown me that thinking in a nonsensical way can be quite liberating—if only I could rhyme like him!

David Sedaris, a brilliant writer who has had me laughing since I first picked up Holidays on Ice, and, unbeknownst to him, has helped me believe I could do this. Sure, he only met me once at a book signing; there is no real connection, but let's pretend I had an impact on his life too, right? Thank you, Mr. Sedaris; your reach is far and wide, like a literary GPS that guides me to humor.

Another person I dedicate this book to is Bill Maher because we really need more people like him. His wit and jaded perspective are unmatched by anyone. He's like a verbal Swiss Army knife. Odd as it sounds, he was on my mind often while writing this book. Not sure why, but hey, there you go. Thanks, Mr. Maher, for being the comedian we didn't know we needed but can't live without.

I couldn't go forward without mentioning Dr. Aaron Beck, whose work taught me how powerful our thoughts truly are and that we are in charge of those thoughts, feelings, and behaviors. As his theory simply states: I think, therefore I feel, and as a result, I behave. Seems simple, right, it is NOT! But it changed everything for me, and became my personal reminder that if I can change my thoughts, I can change my life. Through his work, my clients have found success, and so have I.

Dr. Terry Libkuman, a professor who taught me to PRESS ON despite tough times. Yes, I stole his words, and now it's my signature close for anything I write. Many students tell me it inspires them to keep going. Guess what? It's pretty inspiring to me too!

Finally, this book is dedicated to all my clients, students, and readers for engaging with the notion of nonsensical thinking to improve their lives... YOU WILL PREVAIL.
Thank you, one and all!
Press on,
dr. j

Acknowledgments

This is really very difficult to write—harder than deciding whether pineapple belongs on pizza. (It does, fight me.) There are so many people who have encouraged me to go forward with my curious book filled with nonsensical quips, beginning with many of my clients whom I talk with regularly. Though I can't share their names, they've each played a role in shaping my perspective and inspiring my words. Our conversations are filled with insight, honesty, and, at times, much-needed laughter. I want you all to know this:

Life has twists and turns, ups and downs,
Smiles and struggles, laughs and frowns.
The key is to see the bright side shine,
Be a little silly from time to time.
Don't take it so seriously, let worries flow,
Enjoy the moments, let happiness grow.
For life's too short to dwell in strife,
Embrace the joy, and live a content life!

Now, on to some incredible people who deserve more than just a mention (but, alas, I can't afford gold-plated trophies just yet).

First, my niece Miranda Mask, a wonderfully delightful and talented young woman. Thank you, Miranda! I truly appreciate all your help and support... it has made such a difference for me. Without you, I'd probably still be staring at a blinking cursor, wondering if this book was a fever dream.

Then there's Greenville Jayne Wagner, a friend for many decades, in my ear like an encouraging but slightly mischievous Jiminy Cricket. Always pushing me forward, sharing ideas, helping with edits, and reading voraciously (seriously, I think she might be part book at this point). A true friend and chosen sista' for life.

A newer friend, but one who has walked many difficult roads and still manages to be one of the most upbeat and positive humans I've ever met—Rhonda Gravedoni, never forgotten. If resilience were a sport, she'd have a trophy case bigger than my bookshelf.

Of course, I cannot forget Joy Bjerke, the Jaded Mathematician—encouraging, supportive, and an absolute smart-ass (which, let's be honest, is a crucial role in my life). She really wants me to reach my goal of selling a million books—not just to help people think in a more positive manner, but also because, let's face it, she wants an indoor horse arena out of the deal. Dream big, sista', Dream big!

About the Author

JoLene Klumpp, aka dr. j, holds a PhD in Psychology, an MA in Counseling, and a BS in Psychology because she figured one degree was great, but three would really keep things interesting. She currently works as a therapist Online and runs her own private practice, You Matter Therapy, where her mission is simple: help everyone who needs it. To make therapy accessible, she offers a "pay-what-you-can" plan because mental health shouldn't come with a price tag that causes more stress.

When she's not helping people untangle their thoughts, dr. j moonlights as an adjunct professor at the University of Arizona Global Campus, bringing her real-world experience into the (virtual) classroom. Before academia, she spent 22 years in human services, directing employment training programs and working in both state prisons and county jails, which, as you might imagine, gave her plenty of insight into human behavior (it's complicated).

dr. j eventually traded in prison walls for lecture halls, and in 2004, she began working full time as a psychology and human services professor. She's earned Teacher of the Year, the Golden Apple Award, and multiple awards for Excellence in Teaching—which means students actually liked her, a rare feat in higher education! She's taught at various universities and community colleges, often earning tenure before her wanderlust kicked in, leading her to pack up and start fresh at a new institution.

Beyond academia and therapy, dr. j once had a column in the *Clare County Review called Backyard Miracles,* where she highlighted random acts of kindness that people performed without expecting anything in return—because, believe it or not, good people still exist! Her goal is to spread these everyday miracles on social media, proving that kindness is contagious (in a good way, not like the flu). Hopefully, coming soon.

Don't beat yourself up. Stay in touch.
The things that make you dance deserve
a second glance.

Be kind to yourself and give yourself grace.
You're the ace who will win your race.

4

What you're feeling is valid—no need for
a word salad. Keep it simple:
show your dimples and share your giggles.
It's the way to a better day!

6

Let's explore that thought a little more.
Close a door, open a door, and keep your
feet on the floor.

*****

It's okay to take things one step at a time.
Move down the road slowly
but surely, and you'll no doubt land just in
time to spin a fun rhyme.

8

You don't have to have it all
figured out right now.
Take your time. One minute,
three minutes, fifteen minutes—you vow,
and won't you be jiggered to discover
you know how.

*****

Holding onto the past is heavy and bulky.
Let it go so you're free to grow like a tree.
You won't sulk; instead, you'll walk like
the Hulk and plant a seed.
Who knows whoever you'll be?

You figure your trigger has a gripper
you can't shake, but I'm pretty sure
it's really a zipper you can easily take.
With hard work and hope, you'll break that
trigger, and surely you'll know when
you have crawled out of that zipper.

12

Mindfulness reduces woefulness.
Be mindful, or you'll get into a bindful.
Don't get trapped by conflict and worry.
Evict those feelings and embrace the glory.

*****

Don't cry in your beer.
Get rid of the tears. Be fearless.
Embrace your weirdness and tweak your geek.
Don't wait till next week—do it now,
I'll show you how.

14

Comb your hair, climb some stairs, take some action. Action precedes motivation. One action now, two actions tomorrow, and by next week, your feet will be in motion to shatter the bonds that drive your notions.

****

Nobody's perfect, though some try to be, working and working till they're brought to their knees. Living with frustration, exhaustion, and fatigue will remove any chance for happiness and glee.

16

Boundaries in place give you power indeed, to look after your wants and your needs. It just so happens, when you're in control, you'll jump right out of that black hole and see how much happier you will be.

18

Trees are the best—I don't say this in jest. They are rooted in dirt right down to their tips. But you are not planted, or bonded, or stuck. You have the range and the power to change, to flip, to zip, and to rearrange your brain!

*****

Expectations can be tricky when they are marred,
They lead to disappointment and leave you scarred.
When too broad, they set you adrift,
When shortsighted, they cause a rift.
Instead, embrace life and set yourself free,
You are only human—and that's a great place to be.

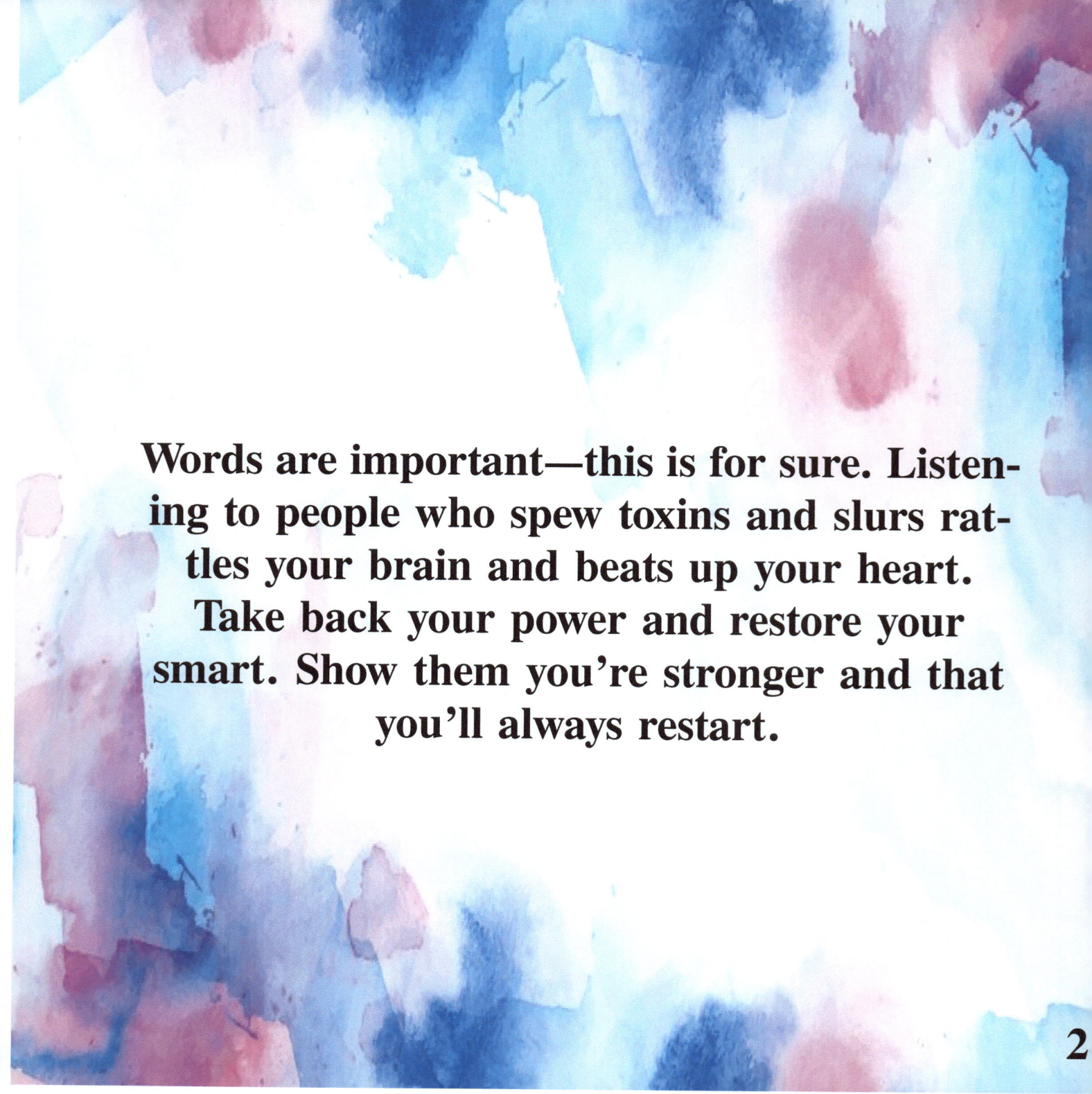

Words are important—this is for sure. Listening to people who spew toxins and slurs rattles your brain and beats up your heart. Take back your power and restore your smart. Show them you're stronger and that you'll always restart.

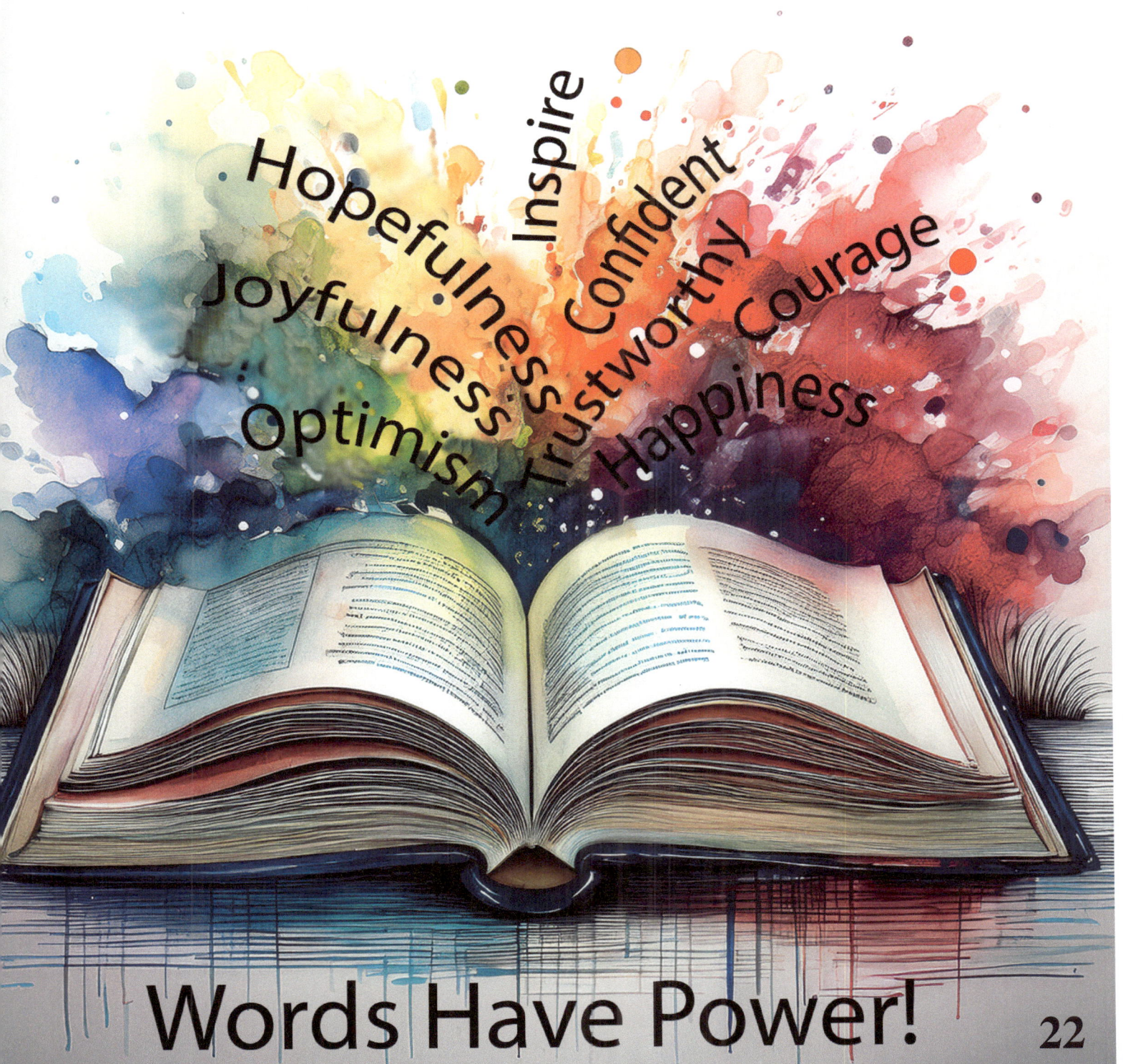

Words Have Power!

22

Living in the moment is the best way to be. If you don't, you'll miss life's melody.

The past is gone, the future's unknown. Here and now is where seeds are sown.

24

Healing is not linear, and that's okay.
Though peculiar, it doesn't mean delay.
Moving forward in any direction you choose
will help you to fight those incoming blues.
Sing a song, tell a joke, do a dance, play a
note, and soon you'll discover you've healed
your bruise.

No deception, dishonesty, or swearing will do. You get to choose what your brain will brew. Try reflection, sincerity, and caring—they're true. And watch as the world shows kindness to you.

You can be amazing—it's about reappraising. Use that brain to avoid going insane. Start at the beginning, and you'll be winning. You'll gain understanding and start counteracting negative thoughts that are trapping and zapping the really big you, who is truly enchanting.

*****

It's important to pay it forward indeed. I can see the benefits are more than you can believe. The rewards are precious and will certainly exceed a day filled with sadness and adversity. Hold out your hand and say, "I can help." Remember, everyone needs relief to melt all those daily troubles we cannot foresee.

28

Dogs are companions that stand by our side,
whether we're happy or lost in our pride.
They ask for so little—just love for a while.
With a wag and a shake, they'll surely make
you smile.
Every moment, they're loyal and they're true—a
friend for all seasons, forever with you.

Don't fret about what you can't control. I bet if you do, you'll end up down a black hole. A place filled with regret, guilt, and shame. Instead, you need to forget and reframe. Think of the possibilities and opportunities ahead. This will surely spread to your future and remove your dread.

Acceptance is lovely—yes, I can see. Compassion for others is necessary.
But acceptance for you is also key if you are ever to be happy.

34

You have the power and the game to rewire those thoughts that result in disdain.
Working hard takes hours and hours for sure, but if you keep going, it will all be a blur.
And oh, how surprised you'll be to find you kicked out shame in the nick of time.

Anger, rage, and wrath are unkind. Engaging creates a commotion that's blind. You'll be fearful, frightful, and spiteful to most, and though it's uncanny, it is you. You'll recognize that it is unhealthy, unhappy, and needs to apologize.

Projection, in a word, is quite absurd. You point your finger and you blame, but the truth of the matter is it's you who needs to be shamed.

38

I don't care what others think of me. If I am being the best of me, I walk my own path, daring and free. True to my heart is all I need to be.

40

Normal is the cycle on the washing machine. No need for you to trifle or change your routine. Consider that you're unique, extraordinary, and original—that's what makes you an irreplaceable individual.

Expectations are troubling at best. They push and pull you and cause you distress. Through many observations, I have found that expectations tend to bring you down. Disappointment sets in, and you brace for the worst, twisting and turning until you feel you will burst.

Instead, consider life filled with surprise, glitter, and wonder at what you will find when you kick expectations out for the very last time.

44

Fear is scary—there is no doubt. It makes you shiver and really stressed out. Confront it directly and reroute. Your thinking can deliver a whole new sprout. Courage and certainty bud into clout, then you'll hammer that fear right out

FEARS

Beliefs that are false are aggravating and irritating.
They toy with your mood and play with your brain until you think you'll go insane. Because they're baiting and escalating, it's important to ensure you are liberating your logic and reason for a headspace that's elevating.

You might lament that you're alone and forgotten,
blanked out and grumbling that you're feeling
rotten.
You moan and groan that it's unfair
because you just want someone to care.
So retrain your brain and dare to shrink
the negative way that you think.

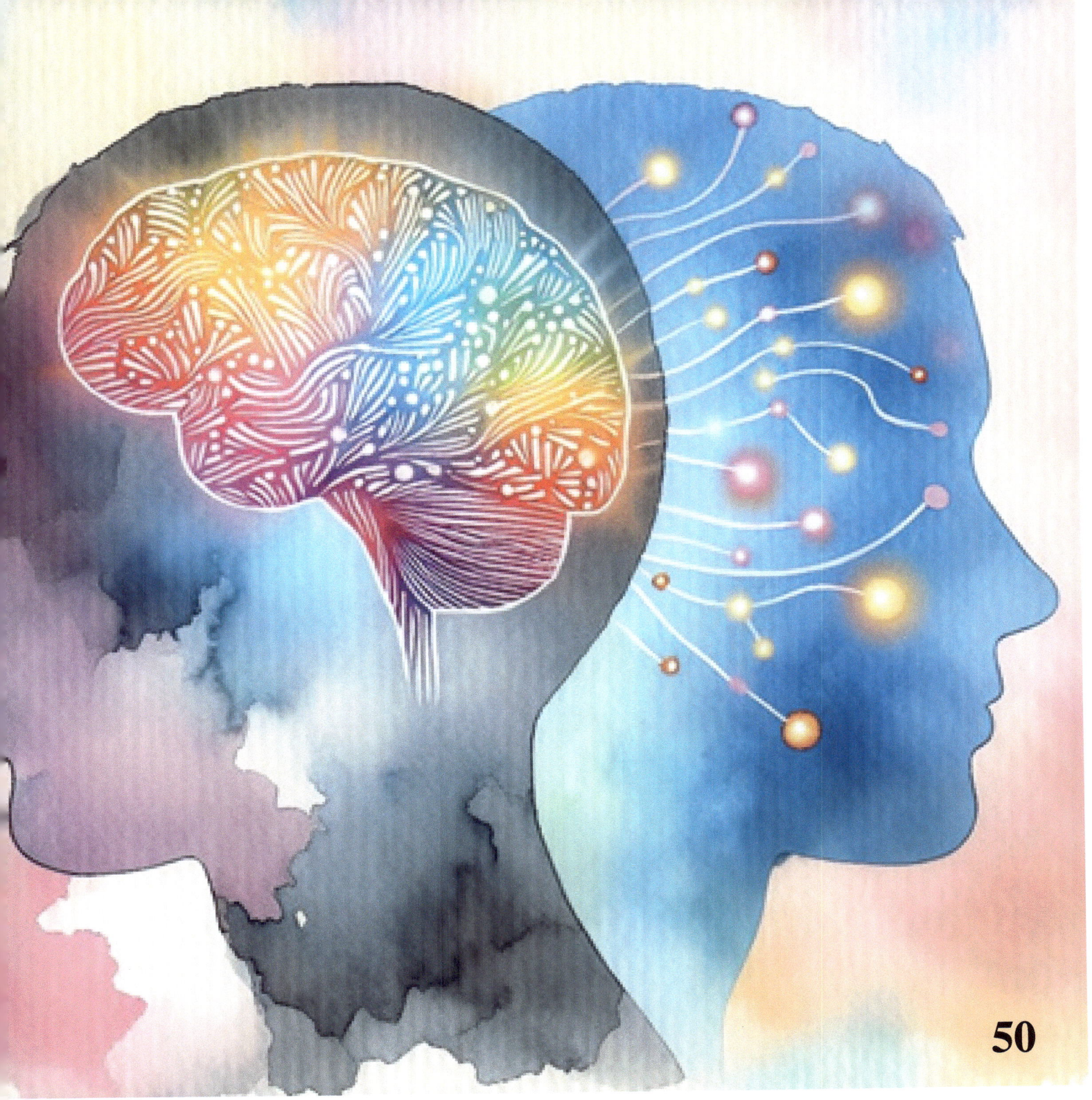

Growth takes time, and it's okay. A tree didn't get its size in a day.
Humans are different in almost every way. You grow in stages, is what they say.
You stumbled, tumbled, and pushed ahead, navigating a world that filled you with dread.
But don't retreat or accept defeat. You're unique in your own way.
Embrace who you are, stand on both feet, and choose a path that keeps you upbeat.

52

Being productive builds confidence to take on anything.
Be sure to be constructive and do the right thing.

*****

Helping hands, a community, a coalition of hope.
As a band, we expand our scope.
We form a new troupe and help others cope,
And what I know for sure is, you yourself will not mope or be a dope.
Instead, you'll find intrinsic rewards that set you on the upslope.

54

Everyone has a piece of the puzzle.
If I exclude one person from my bubble,
I'll end up with a hole in my puzzle.
I would rather be inclusive and chuckle.

Pulled and pushed in a thousand directions,
Rattles my brain and creates millions of ques-
tions.
The trick is to focus on the moment you're in.
It will come together if you breathe and grin
And begin to figure out, right here and now,
The direction you'll steer your ship and how.
You'll be comfortable with what you vow.

Adulthood is where sometimes you're dismayed,
And then you find that you lost your way.

The beauty of humans is they can begin again.
Smile, dance, change your thinking, and grin.
You'll learn how to tumble, scramble, and play,
Like when you were a kid—you'll find another
way.

Family can be tough.
There is so much stuff.
You sort through arguments,
There are so many sentiments.
Thoughts that make you sad,
And thoughts that make you glad.
But you choose to be snappy or happy—
It's up to you to see a new view.

*****

When you're feeling stuck and stressed,
Look for thoughts that are in jest!
With twists and turns both wild and free,
It helps you think nonsensically!

When you think from a more positive perspective,
You can be more introspective and
reflective,
Which leads to a mindset, bright
and inventive,
Making your life more joyful,
bold, and effective.

64

Remember, when we think, we
feel, then act,
Shift your thoughts quick and
stay on track.
In just a blink, you'll spark
new brain waves
That'll lead you to a better way
to start your day.

*****

Don't seal the deal with negatives.
Instead, think about the positives.
You'll learn to be happy and unafraid.
It's you who makes your lemonade.

66

Thinking you're not good enough
Hurts you and puts you in handcuffs.
There is another way to feel—
Changing your thoughts seals the deal.
It's your brain at play, so take control,
Give up the comparative role.
You'll see the positives start to grow,
And exciting brain waves will surely flow!

It doesn't matter if you're
different than most,
No need to be a ghost—take a
moment and boast.
You are unique, and you have
lots to toast.

*****

Look at the beauty of the true you.
Ignore what others say and spew.
They don't really have a clue.